WITHDRAWN

A BRANCH OF MAY

A BRANCH OF MAY
POEMS BY LIZETTE
WOODWORTH REESE

PORTLAND MAINE
THOMAS B MOSHER
MDCCCCIX

CONTENTS

CONTENTS

A BRANCH OF MAY

Another rhymer?   quoth the World.
Faith, these folk be mad!

BETRAYED

HE is false, O Death, she is fair !
   Let me hide my head on thy knee;
Blind mine eyes, dull mine ears, O Death !
   She hath broke my heart for me !

Give me a perfect dream ;
   Find me a rare, dim place ;
But let not her voice come nigh,
   And keep out her face — her face !

THE DESERTED HOUSE

THE old house stands deserted, gray,
　　With sharpened gables high in air,
And deep-set lattices, all gay
　　With massive arch and framework rare;
And o'er it is a silence laid,
That feeling, one grows sore afraid.

The eaves are dark with heavy vines;
　　The steep roof wears a coat of moss;
The walls are touched with dim designs
　　Of shadows moving slow across;
The balconies are damp with weeds,
Lifting as close as streamside reeds.

The garden is a loved retreat
　　Of melancholy flowers, of lone
And wild-mouthed herbs, in companies sweet,
　　'Mid desolate green grasses thrown;
And in its gaps the hoar stone wall
Lets sprays of tangled ivy fall.

The pebbled paths drag, here and there,
　　Old lichened faces, overspun
With silver spider-threads — they wear
　　A silence sad to look upon:

4

It is so long since happy feet
Made them to thrill with pressure sweet.

'Mid drear but fragrant shrubs there stands
   A saint of old made mute in stone,
With tender eyes and yearning hands,
   And mouth formed in a sorrow lone;
'Tis thick with dust, as long ago
'Twas thick with fairest blooms that grow.

Swallows are whirring here and there;
   And oft a little soft wind blows
A hundred odors down the air;
   The bees hum 'round the red, last rose;
And ceaselessly the crickets shrill
Their tunes, and yet, it seems so still.

Or else, from out the distance steals,
   Half heard, the tramp of horses, or
The bleak and harsh stir of slow wheels
   Bound cityward; but more and more,
As these are hushed, or yet increase,
About the old house clings its peace.

A SONG

THE year's a little older grown;
    And fair white boughs by green ways blown
In these new days are no more known.
   (Oh, who can bring the May again?)

And we are wiser grown, we two.
Our story's told; each word was true;
And you love me, and I love you.
   (Oh, who can bring the May again?)
Was it not sweeter ere we knew?
Yet who can bring the May again?

HALLOWMAS

YOU know, *the year's not always May* —
   Oh, once the lilacs were ablow !
  (In truth, not very long ago),
But now, dead leaves drop down the way.

But now, chrysanthemums are gay,
  And some last roses redly glow.
You know, *the year's not always May* —
  Oh, once the lilacs were ablow !

These be the days, this weather gray,
  We think of those we lovèd so ;
  Sweet souls, who heard Death calling low,
And followed him from dark to day.
You know, *the year's not always May*.

A SPINNING SONG

HOW many lilies be ablow?
   Count them and see —
Seven by the wall, and seven by the door;
   'Tis time he came to me.
         Oh, love 's bitter!

Was ever a whiter web than this
   That I spin to-day?
A wedding gown or a winding sheet,
   Love, which shall it be?
         Oh, love 's bitter!

The old dames stand in the street,
   'Neath the willow trees;
And they mark how white my lilies blow,
   And they hear my bees.
         Oh, love 's bitter!

And one dame says, "Five lads of mine
   Be in the sea;"
Another says, "That lad of mine,
   He came not back to me."
         Oh, love 's bitter!

The willow trees grow down to the wharves,
   Green as of old;

8

(Green as the day he went from me;)
  The sea is of gold.
        Oh, love's bitter!

Two ships I see: one in the west —
  Love, is it thine?
One in the east, in a windy mist —
  Oh, love, which is thine?
        Oh, love's bitter!

Then speak the dames: "Her ship went down
  That night at sea."
My seven white lilies — do ye hear?
  For this they speak of me!
        Oh, love's bitter!

9

MY TRUE LOVE LIES ASLEEP

MY true love lies asleep
    In some most heavenly place;
She hath a lily in her hand,
    A smile upon her face.

The dear white roses come
    And climb about her there;
The sweetest winds you ever heard
    Go singing down the air.

The roses climb so high;
    The grasses grow so deep;
You cannot see her where she lies,
    A-smiling in her sleep.

ANNE

(SUDBURY MEETING-HOUSE, 1653)

HER eyes be like the violets,
    Ablow in Sudbury lane;
When she doth smile, her face is sweet
    As blossoms after rain;
With grief I think of my gray hairs,
    And wish me young again.

In comes she through the dark old door
    Upon this Sabbath day;
And she doth bring the tender wind
    That sings in bush and tree;
And hints of all the apple boughs
    That kissed her by the way.

Our parson stands up straight and tall,
    For our dear souls to pray,
And of the place where sinners go,
    Some grewsome things doth say;
Now, she is highest Heaven to me;
    So Hell is far away.

Most stiff and still the good folk sit
    To hear the sermon through;

11

But if our God be such a God,
    And if these things be true,
Why did He make her then so fair,
    And both her eyes so blue?

A flickering light, the sun creeps in,
    And finds her sitting there;
And touches soft her lilac gown,
    And soft her yellow hair;
I look across to that old pew,
    And have both praise and prayer.

Oh, violets in Sudbury lane,
    Amid the grasses green,
This maid who stirs ye with her feet
    Is far more fair, I ween!
I wonder how my forty years
    Look by her sweet sixteen!

A WET JUNE DAY

SCENTS, sounds as of November fill the air;
　　Of myriad blossoms down wet pathways strown,
Of ragged leaves off steaming branches blown
And dropped into dank hollows here and there.
Keen little gusts go whirling through the hush,
Driving the mist before them up the lane.
And lo, the lovely world grows ours again !
The orchard fences, the one elder bush,
Prone with its white face in the thick drenched grass,
The rows of apple trees, gnarled, dripping, sweet,
The highway with its pools agleam like glass;
Then, as still speeds the mist on shining feet,
Meadow, and wood, peaked roofs — beyond
　　　　them shows
A windy west, the color of a rose.

OH, love! Oh, love! this way has hints of you
    In every bough that stirs, in every bee,
Yellow and glad, droning the thick grass through;
In blooms red on the bush, white on the tree:
And when the wind, just now, came soft and fleet,
Scattering the blackberry blossoms, and from some
Fast darkening space that thrush sang sudden sweet,
You were so near, so near, yet did not come!
Say, is it thus with you, oh, friend, this day?
Have you, for me that love you, thought or word?
Do I, with bud or bough, pass by your way;
With any breath of brier, or note of bird?
If this I knew, though you be quick or dead,
All my sad life would I go comforted.

A SONG FOR CANDLEMAS

THERE'S never a rose upon the bush,
   And never a bud on any tree;
In wood and field nor hint nor sign
   Of one green thing for you or me.
Come in, come in, sweet love of mine,
   And let the bitter weather be!

Coated with ice the garden wall;
   The river reeds are stark and still;
The wind goes plunging to the sea,
   And last week's flakes the hollows fill.
Come in, come in, sweet love to me,
   And let the year blow as it will!

SUNRISE

THE east is yellow as a daffodil.
    Three steeples — three stark swarthy
      arms — are thrust
Up from the town. The gnarlèd poplars thrill
Down the long street in some keen salty gust —
Straight from the sea and all the sailing ships —
Turn white, black, white again, with noises sweet
And swift. Back to the night the last star slips.
High up the air is motionless, a sheet
Of light. The east grows yellower apace,
And trembles : then, once more, and suddenly,
The salt wind blows, and in that moment's space
Flame roofs, and poplar-tops, and steeples three;
From out the mist that wraps the river-ways,
The little boats, like torches, start ablaze.

KEATS

FLUTING and singing, with young locks aflow,
   This lad, forsooth, down the long years should
      pass,
With scent of blooms, with daffodils arow,
   Lighting their candles in the April grass.
Ah, 'tis not thus he comes to us, but sweet
   With youth and sorrows!   When we speak
      his name,
Lo, the old house in the old foreign street,
   His broken voice lamenting that his fame
(Alack, he knew not!) passing fleet would be!
   He grieves us with his melancholy eyes.
Yet are all weathers sweeter for that he
   Did sing.   Deep in the Roman dust he lies.
How since he died the century hath sped!—
And they that mocked him, yea, they too are dead.

A THOUGHT OF MAY

ALL that long, mad March day, in the dull town,
    I had a thought of May — alas, alas!
The dogwood boughs made whiteness up and down;
    The daffodils were burning in the grass;
And there were bees astir in lane and street,
    And scent of lilacs blowing tall and lush;
While hey, the wind, that pitched its voice so sweet,
    It seemed an angel talked behind each bush!
The west grew very golden, roofs turned black.
    I saw one star above the gables bare.
The door flew open.   Love, you had come back.
    I held my arms; you found the old way there.
In its old place you laid your yellow head,
    And at your kiss the mad March weather fled!

DOUBT

CREEDS grow so thick along the way,
  Their boughs hide God; I cannot pray.

TRUTH

THE old faiths light their candles all about.
  But burly Truth comes by and blows
    them out.

A DECEMBER ROSE

A ROSE is a rose all times of the year.
  I have one out in my garden there,
In the deep grass out by the gray old stair —
A breath of June in December drear.

Ah, but its red is a little sere,
And nipped by the frost in last night's air!
A rose is a rose all times of the year.
I have one out in my garden there.

So, when Love comes, he is counted dear,
With his reed at his lips, in June-tide fair,
A-piping sweet, or with wind-blown hair,
And tears in his eyes in December drear.
A rose is a rose all times of the year.

A SONG

O LOVE, he went a-straying,
    A long time ago!
I missed him in the Maying,
    When blossoms were of snow;
So back I came by the old sweet way;
    And for I loved him so,
I wept that he came not with me,
    A long time ago!

Wide open stood my chamber door,
    And one stepped forth to greet;
Gray Grief, strange Grief, who turned me sore
    With words he spake so sweet.
I gave him meat; I gave him drink;
    (And listened for Love's feet).
How many years?   I cannot think;
    In truth, I do not know —
    A long time ago!

O Love, he came not back again,
    Although I kept me fair;
And each white May, in field and lane,
    I waited for him there!
Yea, he forgot; but Grief stayed on,
    And in Love's empty chair
Doth sit and tell of days long gone —
    'Tis more than I can bear!

MID-MARCH

IT is too early for white boughs, too late
   For snows.   From out the hedge the wind lets fall
A few last flakes, ragged and delicate.
Down the stripped roads the maples start their small,
Soft, 'wildering fires.   Stained are the meadow stalks
A rich and deepening red.   The willow tree
Is woolly.   In deserted garden-walks
The lean bush crouching hints old royalty,
Feels some June stir in the sharp air and knows
Soon 'twill leap up and show the world a rose.

The days go out with shouting; nights are loud;
Wild, warring shapes the wood lifts in the cold;
The moon's a sword of keen, barbaric gold,
Plunged to the hilt into a pitch black cloud.

THE SINGER

WITH spices, wines and silken stuffs,
    The stout ship sailèd down,
And with the ship the singer came
    Unto the old sea town.

"Peace to ye!" quoth the sailor folk,
    "A month and more have we
Been listening to his songs.   Ah, God!
    None sings so sweet as he."

Up from the wharves the salt wind blew,
    And filled the steep highway;
Seven slender plum trees caught the sun
    Within a courtyard gray.

Out came the daughter of the king;
    Oh, very fair was she!
She was the whitest bough a-grow,
    So fair, so fair was she!

The singer sang, "My love," he sang,
    "Is like a white plum tree!"
Then silence fell on house and court;
    No other word sang he.

The king's daughter, when she was old,
　Sat in a broidered gown,
And spun the flax from her fair fields —
　Oh, it was sweet in town!

Seven plum trees stood down in the court,
　Each one was white as milk;
The king's daughter rose softly there,
　Rustling her broidered silk.

"Oh, set the wheel away, my maids,
　And sing that song to me
The singer sang!" "My love," sang they,
　"Is like a white plum tree!"

SWEET WEATHER

NOW blow the daffodils on slender stalks,
    Small keen quick flames that leap up in the mold,
And run along the dripping garden-walks :
Swallows come whirring back to chimneys old.

Blown by the wind, the pear-tree's flakes of snow
Lie heaped in the thick grasses of the lane ;
And all the sweetness of the Long Ago
Sounds in that song the thrush sends through the rain.

IN JUNE

With a Difference.
HAMLET.

WHO saw the June come? Wel-a-day!
　　My neighbor's bushes, one and all,
And grew white after God's old way,
　　Behind the garden wall.

Who saw the June come? Nay, not she,
My neighbor's daughter, slim and shy,
Long since she left her father's house,
　　Ere yet the rose was nigh.

Last year, last year, there in the sun
She stood and smiled. I did not know
Which was the whitest thing in June,
　　She, or that bush a-grow.

But now; ah, now; yea, now 'tis plain!
When folk be dead, how wise we be!
God's boughs were black beside her snow;
　　Ah, now; yea, now I see!

My neighbor's bushes blow, blow, blow,
And blow about his silent door!
Ye call that white? Nay, 'tis not so;
　　June has been here before.

26

Ye cannot mock me, blossoms sweet;
I know too well your looks of yore;
My neighbor knows (yet blow, blow, blow),
  June has been here before.

AFTER THE RAIN

DRIPPING the hollyhocks beneath the wall,
  Their fires half quenched, a smouldering red ;
A shred of gold upon the grasses tall,
  A butterfly is hanging dead.

A sound of trickling waters, like a tune
  Set to sweet words ; a wind that blows
Wet boughs against a saffron sky ; all June
  Caught in the breath of one white rose.

A RHYME OF DEATH'S INN

A RHYME of good Death's inn!
   My love came to that door;
And she had need of many things,
  The way had been so sore.

My love she lifted up her head,
  "And is there room?" said she;
"There was no room in Bethlehem's inn
  For Christ who died for me."

But said the keeper of the inn,
  "His name is on the door."
My love then straightway entered there:
  She hath come back no more.

THE DEATH POTION

[IN ITALY, 15 —]

ONE drop of this, and she will not know
    If she be foul or fair;
One drop, and I may bind him again
    With a thread of my golden hair.
      (Hear, Lord Jesus!)

I would that those folk across the street,
    In old St. Simon's there,
Would hush their noise: for they sing so sweet
    They make this rare drop seem less rare.
      (Hear, Lord Jesus!)

It is May; my plum trees five
    Down in the court below
Look like five little chorister boys
    Tiptoe to chant, so white they blow.
      (Hear, Lord Jesus!)

And a butterfly like a violet
    Flits through the sun and lights on the sill
Close to my hand.   Are the bees about,
    Or is it the wind comes down the hill?
      (Hear, Lord Jesus!)

But what have *I* to do with the May,
  Or any other weather?
Or with five white plum trees?   Hate and I,
  And I and Hell, be yoked together.
      (*Hear, Lord Jesus!*)

(One drop is sure to kill.)   When she dies,
  They will put the cross on her breast,
And get the golden candlesticks out
  For her head and feet, and call her blest.
      (*Hear, Lord Jesus!*)

But she is a thief! Do ye hear me in Heaven?
  Her soul shall *not* come in
To those white souls.   She is pitch, not snow.
  Saint Simon, Saint Simon, is Theft not sin?
      (*Hear, Lord Jesus!*)

For he was mine, and I was his;
      (*Hear, Lord Jesus!*)
Though we had shame, yet had we bliss.
      (*Hear, Lord Jesus!*)

I fell, but for love, love, love;
  And for love, love, love, I swear!
I, for this man and my love,
  Would have wiped his feet with my hair!
      (*Hear, Lord Jesus!*)

31

This robber came; she lay in wait;
  She sprang upon him unaware;
He thinks to wed her with a ring
  To-morrow in St. Simon's there.
        (*Hear, Lord Jesus !*)

One drop? *And she shall have it then*
  In a sup of her lover's wine ;
So — old things will come back again,
  And I be his, and he be mine !
        (*Hear, Lord Jesus !*)

BLACKBERRY BLOSSOMS

'LONG sunny lane and pike, white, delicate,
   The blackberry blossoms are ablow, ablow,
Hiding the rough-hewn rails 'neath drift of snow,
Fresh-fallen, late. The opening pasture gate
Brushes a hundred of them loose, and shakes
Them down into the tall delicious grass:
Sometimes a little sudden wind doth pass,
And all the air is full of flying flakes.
It seems but yesterday they blew as sweet
Down old school ways, and thrilled me with delight;
And reaching out for them, I heard the fleet,
Glad creek go spinning o'er its pebbles bright.
Ah, well! Ah, me! Even now, long as they last,
I am a child again; Joy holds me fast.

SUNSET

IN the clear dusk upon the fields below,
    The blossoming thorn-bush, white, and
        spare, and tall,
Seems carved of ivory 'gainst the dark wall :
Shut from the sunset sharp the farm-roofs show.
But here upon this height, the straggling hedge
Burns in the wind, and is astir with bees ;
The little pool beneath the willow trees,
Yellow as topaz flames from edge to edge ;
A line of light the deserted highway glows.
Odors like sounds down the rich air do pass,
Spice from each bough, musk from the brier rose
Dropping its five sweet petals on the grass.
Swallows are whirring black against the blaze ;
I hear the creek laugh out from pebbly ways.

THE DEAD SHIP

A KELTIC LEGEND

THE ship came sailing, sailing,
   Into our old town —
My love combed out her golden hair;
   It fell to the hem of her gown.
     Oh, my heart, break!

No master and no crew was hers,
   A ship of the dead was she,
And sailing, sailing, sailing —
   The folk ran out to see.
     Oh, my heart, break!

And first they said nor yea, nor nay;
   Then some began to weep;
And some did count their little lads,
   As a shepherd counts his sheep.
     Oh, my heart, break!

Oh, sailing, sailing, sailing —
   "Whom will it be?" said they;
"She never sails to this our town
   But one doth go away."
     Oh, my heart, break!

35

"Yea, one will go from this our town
    And come back nevermore;
Whate'er His will, Lord God is good;"
    Thus I at my love's door.
        Oh, my heart, break!

Thereat I turned into the house
    And climbed up my love's stair,
And called her softly — through the dusk
    I saw her golden hair.
        Oh, my heart, break!

Who went away from our old town
    And came back nevermore?
It was my love; she lay there dead
    Upon the chamber floor.
        Oh, my heart, break!

A RHYME FOR JUNE

NOW marshy pools on the road's edge,
  Or creeks that slip 'twixt banks of sedge,
With marigolds be set aflare;
And not a corner south or north,
But there a brier-rose breaks forth,
And bees go droning down the air.

The bramble now begins to blow,
The elder-bush puts on its snow,
And birds be sweet till fall of dew;
And when my love and I go out,
So thick the grass grows all about—
In truth, it scarce will let us through.

AUGUST

NO wind, no bird.   The river flames like brass.
        On either side, smitten as with a spell
Of silence, brood the fields.   In the deep grass,
Edging the dusty roads, lie as they fell
Handfuls of shriveled leaves from tree and bush.
But 'long the orchard fence and at the gate,
Thrusting their saffron torches through the hush,
Wild lilies blaze, and bees hum soon and late.
Rust-colored the tall straggling brier, not one
Rose left.   The spider sets its loom up there
Close to the roots, and spins out in the sun
A silken web from twig to twig.   The air
Is full of hot rank scents.   Upon the hill
Drifts the noon's single cloud, white, glaring, still.

EARLY SEPTEMBER

THE swallows have not left us yet, praise God !
    And bees still hum, and gardens hold the musk
Of white rose and of red ; firing the dusk
By the old wall, the hollyhocks do nod,
And pinks that send the sweet East down the wind.
And yet, a yellowing leaf shows here and there
Among the boughs, and through the smoky air —
That hints the frost at dawn — the wood looks thinned.
The little half-grown sumachs, all as green
As June last week, now in the crackling sedge,
Colored like wine burn to the water's edge.
We feel, at times, as we had come unseen
Upon the aging Year, sitting apart,
Grief in his eyes, some ache at his great heart.

A NOVEMBER AFTERNOON

THE long and sad week's wind, like any child,
　　Has sobbed itself to sleep.　This morning's rain
Has strewn the stairway with the petals wild,
Red, ragged, of my sweet last rose.　The lane
Shows me the poplar tree, blackened and bare,
Clasped to its heart a dangling empty nest.
A few dull yellow leaves stir here and there,
And all the air is clear from east to west.
The year, I think, lies dreaming of the May,
As old men dream of youth, that loved lost thing.
A spring-like thrill is in this weather gray.
I wait to hear some thrush begin to sing;
And half expect, as up and down I go,
To see my neighbor's cherry-boughs ablow!

THE FIRST SNOW

THE dogwood has its bloom again;
    Each blade of grass out in the lane
A little scentless bud doth bear;
The shriveled shrubs to left and right
Let loose a myriad petals light
    To every breath that stirs the air.

Still as in June its briers beneath
The meadow brook shows its white teeth.
    Remembering June, the wild rose-bush
Holds still a berry here and there,
Setting the blackened twigs aflare
    With scarlet in the frosty hush.

Long are the hours from dusk to dawn;
From dawn to dusk — ah, too soon gone!
    Lo, when the brief day sinks to rest,
Then bough by bough, like bone by bone,
The naked trees stand out alone
    Against the keen gold of the west!

TO HER SWEET EYES

SWEET eyes, sweet eyes, that now be in the dust,
    When *you* I had, the May was May in truth !
The round world wore its white as youth did youth,
Sweet eyes, sweet eyes, that now be in the dust !
Of its old music is the wind's throat bare ;
June is not June ; the rose hath lost its red,
The pink its spice ; the hollyhock is dead ;
There are no lilies blowing anywhere —
And yet, I came upon a grave to-day,
By a church door, and there a thorn-bush stood,
Astir with bees, abrim with blossoms gay,
The one fair thing of field and hedge and wood.
You lay beneath, sweet eyes, sweet eyes and true,
And it was fair because, because of you !

NINE HUNDRED AND FIFTY COPIES OF
THIS BOOK PRINTED ON VAN GELDER
HAND-MADE PAPER AND THE TYPE
DISTRIBUTED.